Servants Heart

From The Voice Of A Volunteer

Jamie Pulos-Fry

There are a lot of practical and helpful lessons underscored here. Thank you for your heart to share with others through your life experiences.
– Mrs. Jill Ghrist, Instructor, West Coast Baptist College, Lancaster, California

I have known Jamie for several years, and I know that she lives what she talks about in this book. She is truly a servant for the Lord and for other people. You will be challenged and blessed by her book.
– Mrs. Suza Rasmussen, Instructor, West Coast Baptist College, Lancaster, California

I appreciate the spirit with which you wrote it, and I trust it will encourage others to find ways to volunteer for the Lord as you have.
– Mr. Jon Guy, Instructor, West Coast Baptist College and Choir Director of Lancaster Baptist Church, Lancaster, California

Jamie is truly a faithful servant in ministry. Her heart to serve and years of experience can be clearly seen within her book. She offers practical pointers for serving faithfully and effectively as a volunteer.
– Mr. Jacob Bundy, Director of Bus, Ministry of Lancaster Baptist Church, Lancaster, California

Dedication

This book is dedicated to a special friend, Jo Ann Eaton.

First, for the great volunteer and servant's heart that she has, for the many times that she picked up and dropped off people at the airport. Plus, she would invite college students to her home for dinner each week.

Second, for the service that she did for the many widows of the church by preparing and servicing a fellowship dinner once a month. Third, by volunteering in the church bookstore and encouraging college students and visitors every week.

Fourth, by using a few of her many gifts: singing in the choir and by preparing the weekly newsletter for her Bible class.

Thank you, special friend, for always being there even when you moved away to live closer to family.

TABLE OF CONTENTS

Foreword

This book came to fruition because I had noticed that where I volunteer we had some issues that need to be addressed.

Plus, I really had not read or seen a book about volunteering in the Christian environment or anywhere for that matter.

I started doing some research on it, and this book is the result of that research from a faithful volunteer.

Acknowledgments

I am thankful to many people for their generous contributions to make this book possible.

First, I'm thankful to Brother Larry Cox and Brother Rick Bishop for their time and work training me in the bookstore and Great Awakening Cafe.

Second, I wish to thank those godly volunteers who have been my examples throughout the years of serving in the college. Many are still encouraging me through their consistent godliness: Mrs. Gerri Siegel, Mr. Don Powers, and Mr. Rich Childress, and so many others.

Third, I would like to thank those who helped with the proofreading, designing, and publishing of this book. It would not have come to be without all their hard work. Thank you.

Fourth, I would like to thank the Lord for giving me the gift of serving others, so I could share with a kind and giving heart in this world.

Thank you. Amen.

Introduction

Does volunteering matter? Yes, it does matter. And although you may have many different reasons and motivations why you volunteer or how you volunteer, there are four overarching benefits that you receive when you volunteer:

1. **You're able to draw closer to God:** When you spend time volunteering to help people, you actually draw closer to Him. You feel more connected to Jesus, and His teachings and the way of life that He practiced and advocated. The Bible shows this in so much of Jesus early life.

2. **You'll know you are making a difference in other people's lives:** By volunteering, you are giving people your time. By giving freely of your time, you know that you are making a positive difference in the lives of others. You can do this by giving freely at church or for the veterans, plus for the men and women that service us and keep us safe from harm every day.

3.   **You are setting a good example for your kids:** When you volunteer on a regular basis, your children grow up understanding the value and importance of helping those who are not as blessed as you are. This is something that I say or think when I have a trial, to remind me of just that. "There is always someone out there that has it worse than I do."

4.   **You grow personally:** When you volunteer, you not only enrich the lives of others around you but also grow personally, both spiritually and socially. You learn more about the world and its ways and you also develop self-confidence and self-esteem, characteristics that help you, no matter where you are.

In the past, it was thought that individuals volunteered strictly for the practice of unselfish concern for the welfare of others (opposed to egoism). Some reasons would be like " the Good Samaritan that goes out of his way to aid a stranger. "Another example would be the soldier who goes back to save a fallen comrade. It was the noble thing for someone to lend a hand for the greater good of mankind. Some people helping those in need for no reward, favor or any show of gratitude.

However, recent studies have indicated that there may be other reasons:

Some people volunteer to gain career experience, to build their resume.

Some people volunteer to build self-esteem, to make themselves feel better. To feel needed. To truly feel like they are making a contribution to society.

Some people volunteer for the social aspect, to climb the social ladder while helping those less fortunate.

Some people volunteer as a result of the instilled set of values they have, set of values that compel them to want to help others.

However, I volunteer to give back to my community. I am grateful for the help I received from others. When I was in high school I participated in the Junior Achievement Program and Letter Girls Club.

Through Junior Achievement Program and Letter Girls Club I was able to acquire skills and opportunities that have helped me become the woman that I am today. So I give back by serving at my church and college to enable kids to have the same chances at life that I have had.

Chapter One

Hebrews 11:6

But without faith *it is* impossible to please *him:* for he that cometh to God must believe that he is, and that he is a rewarder of them that diligently seek him.

Being Faithful

As a volunteer I have begun to understand what it means to be faithful. It's like what a church may have up in their kid's school wall saying WWJD. It means What Would Jesus Do. So think what Jesus would do in this situation. What would Jesus as a volunteer do and say throughout the day to make Him happy.

What faithfulness means to me:

- Show up on time on the days you promised you to be there.
- Do the things they show you and more. Go the extra mile.
- Follow the rules from the boss of the day. Every supervisor and every day or evening is different, person and set up.
- If you cannot come let them know in advance, so they can get someone to cover for you.
- There are times that you may have to do everything by yourself. Do it with joy on your face and in your heart.

What faithfulness means in the Bible:

- That God is constant or faithful in keeping His promises, and therefore is trustworthy and unchangeable in His ethical nature.

It is applied to men in Psalm 101:6 (King James Bible) "Mine eyes *shall be* upon the faithful of the land, that they may dwell with me: he that walketh in a perfect way, he shall serve me." I do understand that we are not perfect like Jesus Christ. I remember when I was in West Coast College Chapel and one of the pastors was teaching us that we have a goal by the time we leave this earth and that is to do our best to be perfect just like Jesus Christ. That we need to grow every day to be just like him.

Jesus shows His gracious promise, in Deuteronomy, that his faithfulness shows in the Old Testament to awaken trust in God. "Know therefore that the LORD thy God, he is God, the faithful God, which keepeth covenant and mercy with them that love him and keep his commandments to a thousand generations;" (Deuteronomy 7:9)

The New Testament teaching concerning faithfulness shows the objects of a confident trust in God. "Ye *are* witnesses, and God also, how holily and justly and unblameably we behaved ourselves among you that believe:" (1 Thessalonians 2:10)

Nehemiah 9:8 it shows a heart which is faithful. "And foundest his heart faithful before thee, and madest a covenant with him to give the land of the Canaanites, the Hittites, the Amorites, and the Perizzites, and the Jebusites, and the Girgashites, to *give it*, I say, to his seed, and hast performed thy words; for thou art righteous:"

Chapter Two

2 Timothy 3:7

Ever learning, and never able to come to the knowledge of the truth.

Romans 15:4

For whatsoever things were written aforetime were written for our learning, that we through patience and comfort of the scriptures might have hope.

Proverbs 1:5

A wise *man* will hear, and will increase learning; and a man of understanding shall attain unto wise counsels:

Willing to Learn Something New

Willing to learn something new means this to me: that you are willing to listen to someone about something that you already know and have experience in. Here are eight things that help me every day when I am serving my church:

- Have an open mind before you try to fix or help with something that just happened and needs your help.

- That you're a people person, fast learning, always willing to work with others if necessary.

- Have a positive attitude that lets you relax, remember, focus, and absorb information as you learn. You're ready to welcome new experiences and recognize many different kinds of learning opportunities. And when you can see opportunities, hope increases.

- Are you willing to make mistakes and learn from them? View failures as feedback that provides you with the information you need to learn and grow every day.

- Match behavior with values. Demonstrate your positive personal values in all that you do and say. Be sincere and real.

- Speak honestly and kindly. Think before you speak.

- Make sure your intention is positive and your words are sincere.

- Take responsibility for your actions, for your thoughts, feelings, and words.

- Be willing to do things differently. Recognize what's not working and be willing to change what you're doing to achieve the team's goal.

Now we are going to look at some of the things Jesus would say and do in the Bible as well as learn something new. He would look into teaching you so you can be a wiser person.

- Proverbs 9:9 "Give instruction to a wise man, and he will be yet wiser: teach a just man, and he will increase in learning."

- Proverbs 12:1 "Whoso loveth instruction loveth knowledge: but he that hateth reproof is brutish."

- Job 34:10, 16, 34 "<u>Therefore hearken unto me you men of understanding: far be it from God,</u> that he should do wickedness; and from the Almighty, that he should commit iniquity. 16 If now thou hast understanding, hear this: hearken to the voice of my words. 34 Let men of understanding tell me, and let a wise man hearken unto me."

- Psalms 119:98-100 "<u>Thou through thy commandments hast made me wiser than mine enemies:</u> for they are ever with me. 99 I have more understanding than all my teachers: for thy testimonies are my meditations. 100 I understand more than the ancients, because I keep thy precepts."

- Proverbs 18:15 "The heart of the prudent getteth knowledge; and the ear of the wise seeketh knowledge."

- Proverbs 10:17 "He is in the way of life that keepeth instruction: but he that refuseth reproof erreth."

- 2 Timothy 2:15 "Study to shew thyself approved unto God, a workman that needeth not to be ashamed, rightly dividing the word of truth."

Chapter Three

Philippians 2:1-5

It there be therefore is any consolation in Christ, if any comfort from love, if any fellowship in the Spirit, if any bowels and mercies, fulfill ye my joy that ye be likeminded, having the same love, being of one accord, of one mind. Let nothing be done through strife or vainglory; but in lowliness of mind let each esteem other better than themselves. Look not every man on his own things, but every man also on the things of others. Let this mind be in you, which was also in Christ Jesus:

Being a Servant

To be a servant we need to be useful for others and God. It is not about pleasing mankind all the time. Yes, God would like us to work well with others and make friends. But he would like us to first follow God's Ten Commandments all the time.

The Ten Commandments (Exodus 20:2-17 KJV)

1

"I am the LORD thy God, which have brought thee out of the land of Egypt, out of the house of bondage. Thou shalt have no other gods before me.

2

"Thou shalt not make unto to thee any graven image, or any likeness of any thing that is in heaven above, or that is in the earth beneath, or that is in the water under the earth: Thou shalt not bow down thyself to them nor serve them: for I the LORD thy God, am a jealous God, visiting the iniquity of the fathers upon the children unto the third and fourth generations of them that hate me; And shewing mercy unto thousands, of them that love me, and keep my commandments.

3

"Thou shalt not take the name of the LORD thy God in vain, for the LORD will not hold him guiltless that taketh his name in vain.

4

"Remember the Sabbath day, to keep it holy. Six days you shalt thou labour, and do all thy work: But the seventh day is the Sabbath of the LORD thy God: in it you shalt not do any work, thou, nor thy son, nor thy daughter, thy manservant, nor thy maidservant, nor thy cattle, nor thy stranger that is within thy gates. For in six days the LORD made heaven and earth, the sea, and all that in them is, and rested the seventh day: wherefore the LORD blessed the sabbath day, and hallowed it.

5

"Honour thy father and thy mother: that thy days may be long upon the land which the LORD thy God giveth thee.

6

"Thou shalt not kill.

7

"Thou shalt not commit adultery.

8

"Thou shalt not steal.

9

"shalt not bear false witness against thy neighbour.

10

"Thou shat not covet thy neighbour's house; thou shalt not covet thy neighbour's wife, nor his manservant, nor his maidservant, nor his ox, nor his ass, nor any thing that is thy neighbour's."

Think before we do and say things to others. Would we like to be treated that way? When you are volunteering for your church or anywhere think about these things and you will be a blessing to others and to God at all times.

Mark 10:42-45

But Jesus called them to *him,* and saith unto them, Ye know that they which are accounted to rule over the Gentiles exercise lordship over them; and their great ones exercise authority upon them. But so shall it not be among you: but whosoever will be great among you, shall be your minister: And whosoever of you will be the chiefest, shall be servant of all. For even the Son of man came not to be ministered unto, but to minister, and to give his life a ransom for many.

We may not be perfect at all times when serving. But our goal is to be like Jesus when we leave this earth.

Chapter Four

1 Thessalonians 5:11-23

11 Wherefore comfort yourselves together, and edify one another, even as also ye do.

Various Exhortations

12 And we beseech you, brethren, to know them which labour among you, and are over you in the Lord, and admonish you; 13 And to esteem them very highly in love for their work's sake. And be at peace among yourselves. 14 Now we exhort you, brethren, warn them that are unruly, comfort the feebleminded, support the weak, be patient toward all men. 15 See that none render evil for evil unto any man; but ever follow that which is good, both among yourselves, and to all men. 16 Rejoice evermore. 17 Pray without ceasing. 18 In everything give thanks: for this is the will of God in Christ Jesus concerning you. 19 Quench not the Spirit. 20 Despise not prophesyings. 21 Prove all things; hold fast that which is good. 22 Abstain from all appearance of evil.

Blessing and Admonition

23 And the very God of peace sanctify you wholly; and I pray God your whole spirit and soul and body be preserved blameless unto the coming of our Lord Jesus Christ.

Being Helpful

Here are some things that I have learned from West Coast Baptist College Chapel. They gave us a bookmark that I keep in my daily journal that goes like this:

12 Ingredients OF ENCOURAGERS
EDIFY
ONE ANOTHER
ENCOURAGE
AUTHORITY
HONOR
OTHERS
BE A
PEACEMAKER
HELP
WEAK
BE
PATIENT
DO
GOOD
REJOICE
PRAY
GIVE
THANKS
OBEY
THE HOLY SPIRIT
ABSTAIN
FROM WRONG APPEARANCES

These have helped me remember what I should be thinking when serving. Am I always perfect at everything? Of course not, but I try to keep things in front of me to help me keep working on them daily.

Chapter Five

1 Timothy 5:1-3

Rebuke not an elder, but intreat *him* as a father; *and* the younger men as brethren;
The elder women as mothers; the younger as sisters, with all purity. Honour widows that are widows indeed.

Hebrews 13:17

Obey them that have the rule over you, and submit yourselves: for they watch for your souls, as they that must give account, that they may do it with joy, and not with grief: for that is unprofitable for you.

Working with Younger People

As we get older we find it harder to work with young people. It is hard to have them teach you and to correct you, but when you really understand who the boss is and that is God, it does not matter anymore. Just learn to humble yourself and then you will realize that you want to do right. For example: sometimes I leave a note for the supervisor so they know that I may have done something wrong so it can be fixed before the close of the day. Then the manager lets me know what I did and how to fix it.

For some of us it is hard to admit that we made a mistake. The bible shows us in a few bible verses how to work on that below: Biblical humility is not only necessary to enter the kingdom, it is also necessary to be great in the kingdom. "But it shall not be so among you: but whosoever will be great among you, let him be your minister; And whosoever will be chief among you, let him be your servant:" (Matthew 20:26-27) Here Jesus is our model. Just as He did not come to be served, but to serve, so must we commit ourselves to serving others in all lowliness of mind, always considering others better than ourselves. *"Let* nothing *be done* through strife or vainglory; but in lowliness of mind let each esteem other better than themselves (Philippians 2:3) This attitude precludes selfish ambition, conceit, and the strife that comes with self-justification and self-defense. The truly humble does not defend himself when falsely accused or unjustly treated. He defends the truth, but not his own ego or reputation. Jesus showed His humility as He washed the disciples' feet in (John 13: 1-16,) "1 Now before the feast of the passover, when Jesus knew that his hour was come that he should depart out of this world unto the Father, having loved his own which were in the world, he loved them unto the end. 2 And supper being ended, the devil having now put into the heart of Judas Iscariot, Simon's *son,* to betray him; 3 Jesus knowing that the Father had given all things into his hands, and that he was come from God, and went to God; 4 He riseth from supper, and laid aside his garments; and took a towel and girded himself. 5 After that he poureth water into a bason, and began to wash the disciples' feet, and to wipe *them* with the towel wherewith he was girded. 6 Then cometh he to Simon Peter: and Peter saith unto him, Lord, dost thou wash my feet? 7 Jesus answered and said unto him, What I do thou knowest not now; but thou shalt know hereafter. 8 Peter saith unto him, Thou shalt never wash my feet. Jesus answered him, If I wash thee not, thou hast no part with me. 9 Simon Peter saith unto him, Lord, not my feet only, but also *my* hands and *my* head. 10 Jesus saith to him, He that is washed needeth not save to wash *his* feet, but is clean every whit: and ye are clean, but not all. 11 For he knew who should betray him; therefore said he, Ye are not all clean. 12 So after he had washed their feet, and had taken his garments, and was set down again, he said unto them, Know, ye what I have done to you? 13 Ye call me Master and Lord: and ye say well; for so I am. 14 If I then, *your* Lord and Master, have washed your feet; ye also ought to wash one another's feet. 15 For I have given you an example, that ye should do as I have done to you. 16 Verily, verily, I say unto you, The servant is not greater than his lord; neither he that is sent greater than he that sent him." (John 13:1-16). "And being found in fashion as a man, he humbled himself, and became obedient unto death, even the death of the cross." (John 13:1-16). "And being found in fashion as a man, he humbled himself, and became obedient unto death, even the death of the cross."(Philippians 2:8). In His humility, He was always obedient to the Father. The humble Christian should also be willing to put aside all selfishness and submit in obedience to God and His Word. True humility produces godliness, contentment, and security.

1 Houdmann, S. Michael, CEO. "What the Bible say about humility?" GotQuestions.org.gotquestions.org/Bible-humility.html. <http://www.gotquestions.org/Biblehumility.html#ixzz3eTRARiEu>.

Chapter Six

1 Peter 5:5

Likewise, ye younger, submit yourselves unto the elder. Yea, all of you be subject one to another, and be clothed with humility: for God resisteth the proud, and giveth grace to the humble.

Ephesians 4:31-32

Let all bitterness, and wrath, and anger, and clamour, and evil speaking, be put away from you, with all malice: 32 And be ye kind one to another, tenderhearted, forgiving one another, even as God for Christ's sake hath forgiven you.

Working with Older People

As younger people it is hard for us to listen to older people. We feel that they do not know what we are going through. Things are different now, things have changed, they cannot teach me anything. But in the long run they can. They can teach you to slow down, look and think before you open your mouth, that you cannot control anything. Only God can. We are so busy running around that we do not see or hear what God is trying to teach or show us every day. We really believe that we do it all by ourselves.

Here are some things that we may want to think about when working with older people:

Exercise Patience and Compassion

It goes without saying that patience and compassion are often needed when dealing with any one as well as older people. Physical challenges, slow movement, forgetfulness, neediness, and apathy are just some of the behaviors you might encounter. Sometimes it's easy to lose patience and become frustrated. Remember this could be you some day and wouldn't you want to be treated kindly?

Asking questions offers the senior a greater sense of **respect** and regard. Offering options gives her or him a greater sense of **control** of the immediate environment. Let them feel they're wanted and part of the decision making process, and that they have a degree of control over some aspects of their lives.

Offer Choices Whenever Possible

Many older adults desire to maintain a sense of independence. This may be especially important when seniors feel their physical and cognitive limitations, but still desire ways to maintain some level of local control in their lives. Whenever possible and appropriate, offer an older adult a choice when interacting with her or him. It could just be asking the senior if they would like to have choice A or choice B for lunch. Having the ability to exercise choice can provide the older adult a greater sense of confidence, esteem, and security, as the senior feels the power to be proactive in life.

I am so glad that God watches out for me and gave me His book to read and teaches me to follow His path and not mine anymore. I may make mistakes weekly, even daily, but God gives me Godly counsel from senior saints, what we call a group of older people at my church. They help me to see things through wiser eyes and open my mind to newer ways of thinking and doing things.

Here are some of the things that the Bible shows us about working with older people:

What does the Bible Say?

1.   1 Timothy 5:1-3 "Rebuke not an elder, but intreat *him* as a father; *and* the younger men as brethren; The elder women as mothers; the younger as sisters, with all purity. Honour widows that are widows indeed." In 1 Timothy it shows us that we should never speak harshly to an older man, but appeal to him respectfully as you would to your own father. Talk to younger men as you would to your own brothers. Treat older women as you would your mother, and treat younger women with all purity as you would your own sisters. Take care of any widow who has no one else to care for her.

2.   Hebrews 13:17 "Obey them that have the rule over you, and submit yourselves: for they watch for your souls, as they that must give account, that they may do it with joy and not with grief: for that *is* unprofitable for you." In Hebrews it tells us to obey your leaders and submit to them, for they are keeping watch over your souls, as those who will have to give an account. Let them do this with joy and

not with groaning, for that would be of no advantage to you.

3.   Job 32: 4 "Now Elihu had waited till Job had spoken, because they *were* elder than he."Now in Elihu he it shows that he had waited before speaking to Job because they were older than he.

4.   Job 32:6 "And Elihu the son of Barachel the Buzite answered and said, I am young, and ye *are* very old; wherefore I was afraid, and durst not shew you mine opinion."Elihu the son of Barachel the Buzite showed that he was young in years, and you are aged; therefore, I was timid and afraid to declare my opinion to you.

God Would Honor them

1.   Leviticus 19:32 "Thou shalt rise up before the hoary head, and honour the face of the old man, and fear thy God: I am the LORD"

2.   1 Peter 5:5 "Likewise, ye younger, submit yourselves unto the elder. Yea, all *of you* be subject one to another, and be clothed with humility: for God resisteth the proud, and giveth grace to the humble."

3.   Exodus 20:12 "Honour thy father and thy mother: that thy days may be long upon the land which the LORD thy God giveth thee."

Listen to their wise words

1.   1 Kings 12:6 "And king Rehoboam consulted with the old men, that stood before Solomon his father while he yet lived, and said, How do ye advise that I may answer this people?" so he asked.

2.   Job 12:12 "With the ancient *is* wisdom; and in length of days understanding." <u>Wisdom is with the aged,</u> and understanding in length of days.

3.   Exodus 18:17-20 "And Moses' father in law said unto him, The thing that thou doest *is* not good. Thou wilt surely wear away, both thou, and this people that *is* with thee: for this thing *is* too heavy for thee; thou art not able to perform it thyself alone. Hearken now unto my voice, I will give thee counsel, and God shall be with thee: Be thou for the people to God-ward, that thou mayest bring the causes unto God: And thou shalt teach them ordinances and laws, and shalt shew them the way wherein they must walk, and the work that they must do."

Helpful Reminders

1.   Matthew 25:40 "And the King shall answer and say unto them, Verily I say unto you, In as much as ye have done *it* unto one of the least of these my brethren, ye have done *it* unto me."

2.   Matthew 7:12 "Therefore all things whatsoever ye would that men should do to you, do ye even so to them: for this is the law and the prophets."

3.   Deuteronomy 27:16 "Cursed be he that setteth light by his father or his mother. And all the people shall say, Amen."

4.   Hebrews 13:16 "But to do good and to communicate forget not: for with such sacrifices God is well pleased." This is saying do not forget to do good and to share with others, for with such sacrifices God is pleased.

Chapter Seven

Galatians 3:28

There is neither Jew nor Greek, there is neither bond nor free, there is neither male nor female: for ye are all one in Christ Jesus.

Deuteronomy 10:17

For the LORD your God is God of gods, and Lord of lords, a great God, a mighty, and a terrible, which regardeth not persons, nor taketh reward:

Showing No Favoritism

We often show favoritism thinking we are helping others or friends in our life. The dictionary says that favoritism is "the favoring of one person or group over other with equal claims: favored - regarded or treated with preference or partiality; enjoying special advantages, privileged."

I see that favoritism is incongruent with God's character: "God does not show favoritism" (Romans 2:11). All are equal before Him. There is no favoritism with in him. (Ephesians 6:9) says, "And, ye masters, do the same things unto them, forbearing threatening: knowing that your Master also is in heaven; neither is there respect of persons with them."

Second, the Bible teaches Christians they are not to show favoritism: "My brethren, have not the faith of our Lord Jesus Christ, the Lord of glory, with respect of persons" (James 2:1).

Third, the Bible calls favoritism a sin: "If you fulfil the; royal law according to the scripture, thou shalt love thy neighbor as thyself,' ye do well. But if ye have respect to persons, ye commit sin, and are convinced of the law as transgressors" (James 2:8-9). Favoritism is a serious offense against God's call to love one's neighbor as oneself.

Here are some of the verses that I have already mentioned and more that we need to look at when we are serving with others and for the Lord, if we want to be a blessing to God and others around us:

James 2:9 - But if ye have respect to persons, ye commit sin, and are convinced of the law as transgressors.

Acts 10:34 - Then Peter opened his mouth, and said, Of a truth I perceive that God is no respecter of persons:

Romans 2:11 - For there is no respect of persons with God.

James 2:1 - My brethren, have not the faith of our Lord Jesus Christ, the Lord of glory, with respect of persons.

Genesis 37:4 - And when his brethren saw that their father loved him more than all his brethren, they hated him, and could not speak peaceably unto him.

Ephesians 6:9 - And, ye masters, do the same things unto them, forbearing threatening: knowing that your Master also is in heaven; neither is there respect of persons with him.

James 2:5 - Hearken, my beloved brethren, Hath not God chosen the poor of this world rich in faith, and heirs of the kingdom which he hath promised to them that love him?

Favoritism is a problem we still deal with every day. Favoritism and partiality are not from God, and Christians are called to love others. As humans, we tend to form judgments based on selfish, personal criteria rather than seeing others as God sees them. May we grow in the grace and knowledge of our Lord and Savior Jesus Christ and follow His example by treating every person the same with God's love (John 3:16).

"For God so loved the world, that he gave his only begotten Son, that whosoever believeth in him should not perish, but have everlasting life."

Chapter Eight

Matthew 7:7

"Ask, and it shall be given to you; seek, and ye shall find; knock, and it shall be opened unto you."

Hebrews 4:15-16

"For we have not have a high priest which cannot be touched with the feeling of our infirmities; but was in all points tempted like as we are, yet without sin. Let us therefore come boldly unto the throne of grace that we may obtain mercy and find grace to help in time of need."

Asking Questions

When I serve at my church I find that every day is different and the best thing for me to do is to ask questions before starting my day. The volunteers that I work with are different each day. The things I work with are different each day. The basics are the same, but the supervisor and the workers are different each day. Each supervisor likes things done a certain way. Rules and guidelines can change at any time as well. It is best to not assume that everything is the same as usual.

As volunteers we are there to help others or make them feel comfortable. We need to be very open to others when answering a question or asking for help about church or the service that we are giving. It is our responsibility to learn and share as much information as we can. That could be finding something or putting something away for someone.

Below are some Bible verse examples about asking for help:

Hebrews 13:5-6
"Let your conversation be without covetousness; and be content with such things as ye have: for he hath said, "I will never leave thee nor forsake thee. "So that we may boldly say, "The LORD is my helper, I will not fear, what man shall do unto me."

Proverbs 3:5-6
"Trust in the LORD with all thine heart; and lean not unto thine own understanding. In all thy ways acknowledge him, and he shall direct thy paths."

Chapter Nine

Habakkuk 1:13

Thou art of purer eyes than to behold evil, and canst not look on iniquity: wherefore lookest thou upon them that deal treacherously, *and* holdest thy tongue when the wicked devoureth *the man that is* more righteous than he?

Isaiah 64:6

For since the beginning of the world *men* have not heard, nor perceived by the ear, neither hath the eye seen, O God, beside thee, *what* he hath prepared for him that waited for him.

Matthew 15:23-24

But he answered her not a word, and he disciples came and besought him, saying, send her away; for she cried after us. But he answered and said, I am not sent but unto the lost sheep of the house of Israel.

Saying No

Knowing who the boss is in our life will help us understand why or when someone tells us no. Our boss is and always will be God, but we always have someone who we need to report to in order to get a job done.

I have learned that saying no does not hurt that much. It just means that I am not doing something the way it should be done in that environment, that I need to learn something new and that it needs to be done a different way this time.

Here are a few Bible verses that will help you about saying no:

Matthew 5:37-39

But let your communication be, Yea, yea; Nay, nay: for whatsoever is more than these cometh of evil. Ye have heard that it hath been said, an eye for an eye, and a tooth for a tooth: But I say unto you, that ye resist not evil: but whosoever shall smite thee on thy right cheek, turn to him the other also.

I Corinthians 10:13

There hath no temptation taken you but such as is common to man: but God *is* faithful, who will not suffer you to be tempted above that ye are able; but will with the temptation also make a way to escape, that ye may be able to bear *it*.

Here are a few times when I have had to say no.

- When you have been told you only have so much and be sparing on what you are giving out.
- When you have returns and that is something   only the manger does, after a certain date.
- When someone wants seconds and you have to tell them to wait until after a certain time period, because we have to make sure everyone gets fed first.

Conclusion

As we have seen, our volunteering can be of value to others and to ourselves. With that in mind, let's take a look at a few ways that an understanding of Gods reasons for volunteering might lead us to the right response.

- **First, in the first chapter, "Being Faithful"**, we learned what it means to be a faithful volunteer. That God is constant in keeping His promises and we should do the same as a volunteer.

- **Second, in Chapter Two, "Willing to Learn Something New",** being willing to do things differently. Recognize what's not working and be willing to change what you're doing to achieve the team's goal.

- **Third, in Chapter Three and Four, "Being a Servant and Being Helpful,"** we need to be useful to others and God. We should keep the Ten Commandments and keep things in front of us to help remember to think like God when we are serving.

- **Fourth, in Chapter Five, "Working with Younger People"**, like it shows by reading Matthew 20:26-27 we need to humble ourselves. "And whosoever will be chief among you, let him be your servant." Jesus is our model. So must we commit ourselves to serving others, always considering others better than ourselves.

- **Fifth, in Chapter Six, "Working with Older People"** teaches that we should exercise patience and compassion, always ask questions; try to offer choices whenever possible. The Bible says that we should never speak harshly to an older person, but appeal to them respectfully as you would to your own or parents.

- **Sixth, in Chapter 7, "Showing No Favoritism"** we see we should be like Jesus in this matter. He is no respecter of persons. Treat everyone equally, and do not give special privileges to anyone. That we should love our neighbor as ourselves. Favoritism is a serious offense against God's call to love one's neighbor as oneself.

- **Seventh, in Chapter 8, "Asking Questions"** we see there are times when things are different and we need to be flexible with people and things around us at all times. Never worry about asking too many questions.

- **Eighth, in Chapter 9, "Saying No"**, here the Lord is teaching us that we are not perfect and that we should be willing to change with the environment and the people around us. That there could be a better way of getting something done and give it a chance.

When I first started writing this book I prayed to God to give me a Christmas song or poem for the back of this book. Then I got up the next morning, with the answer saying, that you do it already. You have been doing it now for many years. So I went, your right it's the Christmas stocking that I bring out every year for the last 3 years. It is something one of my bible teachers asked us to do one year, and I took it another step further.

She asked us to write down what we were thankful for this year and pray over it. But I did more by putting down who I was thankful for and gave it to Baby Jesus every year the night before Christmas. I would put in a Christmas stocking that say's baby Jesus on it and put a running list where I read over the list every year, and would add the new people that were a big blessing to me that year to it.

First it was small poem and asked someone to help me make it into a song. I was told that it needed more lines to the verses. So one day serving in the church bookstore I noticed one plate and one plank with Christmas words that would fix just right for my poem to turn it in to a song.

So that is how the Christmas Stocking came to be in back of this book.

Christmas Stocking

Happy Birthday baby Jesus, the candles are for you, the carols, decorations, the celebrating too, for that one special Christmas stocking that hangs by the fire place so dear. Peace in the world for baby Jesus.

So celebrate the season of Peace and love and joy, remembering the reason is still this baby boy.
Happy Birthday baby Jesus for that one special Christmas stocking that holds all my blessings and gifts from God, those special memories that God brings into our lives every year.
Peace in the world for baby Jesus.

So celebrate the season of Peace and love and joy, remembering the reason is still this baby boy.
Happy Birthday baby Jesus for that one special Christmas list of people past and present that we are thankful for, that is given to baby Jesus, on his birthday every year.
Peace in the world for baby Jesus.

So celebrate the reason for the season, remembering the reason is baby Jesus.
Happy Birthday baby Jesus for all the people that God brings in our lives to encourage us to be thankful for others throughout the year.

Peace in the world for baby Jesus in that one special Christmas stocking that hangs by the fireplace so dear.

Index of Scriptures

About the Author

Jamie Pulos-Fry is a faithful member of Lancaster Baptist Church, Lancaster, California. She likes to serve and volunteer in various areas of the church. Serves in the Coffee Shop and Bookstore for West Coast Baptist College and sings in the Choir at the church, plus was a Captain of a Ladies Bus for 5 years. This is her second book, first one is Encouraging A Friend With Our Trials, and the third one is A WIDOW'S CRY, a helpful tool for widow ministries and she hopes that Servants Heart will be a great help in future volunteering choices in your life.

For more books by
Jamie Pulos-Fry, visit
www.two4avalon.com